How I Found the Lost Atlantis

The Source of All Civilization

By

Paul Schliemann

First published in 1912

Published by Left of Brain Books

Copyright © 2023 Left of Brain Books

ISBN 978-1-397-66633-8

First Edition

All rights reserved. No part of this publication may be reproduced, distributed, or transmitted in any form or by any means, including photocopying, recording, or other electronic or mechanical methods, without the prior written permission of the publisher, except in the case of brief quotations permitted by copyright law. Left of Brain Books is a division of Left Of Brain Onboarding Pty Ltd.

PUBLISHER'S PREFACE

About the Book

"On October 20th, 1912, readers of the New York American were regaled with a startling and perhaps history-making story in a lavish two-page spread. Paul Schliemann, grandson of Heinrich Schliemann, the famous archeologist who excavated Mycenae and the legendary city of Troy, revealed that his grandfather on his deathbed produced a mysterious bequest for any of his heirs willing to devote their life to proving the existence of Atlantis. He claimed that he had spent years following up on this and now was about to produce actual physical evidence of the reality of the fabled lost continent. Or was he....

The New York American was one of the newspapers started by William Randolph Hearst which spawned the term 'Yellow Journalism', the predecessor of such distinguished modern supermarket tabloids such as the National Enquirer. Hearst newspapers could be relied upon for banner headlines, sensational scoops, heart-tugging sob stories, and yarns which skirted the boundaries of good taste, if not logic. So in context, this article, which has occasionally been cited as an actual contribution to the study of Atlantis, can be appreciated as merely a diversion on the level of the Bat Boy or Aliens in the Oval Office.

And indeed, this turned out to be a flash-in-the-pan hoax. There was no follow-up book, and Paul Schliemann dropped out of sight as quickly as he emerged. The promised artifacts were never produced, and scholars who worked closely with Heinrich Schliemann confirmed that he had never demonstrated any interest in Atlantis whatsoever."

(Quote from sacred-texts.com)

CONTENTS

PUBLISHER'S PREFACE
   ATLANTIS 1
   THE NEW DIVING ARMOR 2
   THE OWL-HEADED VASE AND TWO OTHER OBJECTS 3
   SIEGFRIED AND THE DRAGON 4
INTRODUCTION 5
   HOW I FOUND THE LOST ATLANTIS, THE SOURCE OF ALL
   CIVILIZATION 7
   WHAT THE LOST ATLANTIS IS SUPPOSED TO HAVE BEEN 22
   WHO DR. HEINRICH SCHLIEMANN WAS AND THE TREASURES HE
   FOUND 25

ATLANTIS

A Reconstruction of the Lost Continent of Atlantis Made from Deep Sea Surveys by the United States Government. The Gulf Stream Ran About the Continent, Taking Exactly the Same Course as It Does Now, Turning East at the Banks of Newfoundland and Circling on its Way to Europe the Submerged Dolphin Ridge, Which is Evidently a Vestige of the Lost Atlantean Continent. The Concentric Ovals Show How the Great City of the Atlanteans Was Built, According to the Story Told by Plato. There were Three Rings of Canals and Two Zones of Land, Cut by Four Rivers. From This Island Continent, Destroyed Perhaps 20,000 Years Ago, Came All Civilization. Egypt Is Supposed to Have Been Settled by a Colony of Atlanteans, and Also Central and South America.

THE NEW DIVING ARMOR

THE New Diving Armor, Designed by Chevalier Pino to Resist Enormous Water Pressure, Which Will Be Used by the English Expedition Which Has Set Out to Find the Treasures of Atlantis

THE OWL-HEADED VASE AND TWO OTHER OBJECTS

IN the Circle Above Is a Copy of the Ancient Owl-Headed Vase Which Dr. Schliemann Found at Mycenae. The Phoenician Inscription Can Be Seen Above the Owl's Head.

Below It Are Two Other Objects Discovered in the Same Collection and Believed to Have Come from Atlantis.

SIEGFRIED AND THE DRAGON

THE Norse Pantheon and Her oes, Like the Greek, Were Only Memories of Actual Kings, Queens and Heroes of Atlantis, Says Dr. Schliemann. The Siegfried Legend, Like the Greek Legend of Theseus, Is a Real Story of Real Exploits by Real Atlanteans Ages Ago.

INTRODUCTION

DR. Paul Schliemann, the distinguished grandson of the late Dr. Heinrich Schliemann, finder of ancient Troy and one of the world's greatest archaeologists, presentshere one of the most remarkable and fascinating narratives of discovery every published.

Atlantis is the legendary continent mentioned by the Greek philosopher Plato, who in one of his "conversations" told how the priests of the Egyptian Temple of Sais related to Solon, the great lawmaker the story of its destruction about 9000 years B. C. Atlantis, according to this story, was the home of a great civilized race which had conquered and colonized the world. All civilization had come from it.

What is known as the Dolphin Ridge, an enormous submarine plateau, stretching between 25 and 50 degrees north latitude and 20 to 50 degrees west longitude, is supposed to be its sunken remnants. The Azore Islands are believed to be the top of its lofty mountains--all that now remains above water of the lost continent.

If Dr. Paul Schliemann can prove his points the greatest world mystery will have been untangled, the history of our race must be reconstructed and many enigmas will be answered finally.

It is a curious coincidence that at the time Dr. Schliemann is making known his discoveries an expedition is setting out from England to recover treasure from sunken cities in the Bay of

Campeche, off Yucatan. These cities were located by Dr. Ernest Marjolies, after four years in Central America, and he also has evidence which he believes proves them to be part of a colony of Atlantis and sunk in the same convulsion which destroyed the mother country.

Dr. Paul Schliemann's story follows:

HOW I FOUND THE LOST ATLANTIS, THE SOURCE OF ALL CIVILIZATION

by Dr. Paul Schliemann

(Column One)

SOME days before my grandfather, Dr. Heinrich Schliemann, the real discoverer of the great Mycenean civilization whose history is preserved in the books of Homer, died in Naples in 1890, he left a sealed envelope in care of his closest friends. The envelope bore the following inscription: "This can be opened only by a member of my family who solemnly vows to devote his life to the researches outlined therein."

Just an hour before my grandfather died he asked for a piece of paper and asked for a pencil. He wrote with a trembling hand: "Confidential addition to the sealed envelope. Break the owl-headed vase. Pay attention to the contents. It concerns Atlantis. Investigate the east of the ruins of the temple of Sais and the cemetery in Chacuna Valley. Important. Night approaches-- Lebewohl."

He closed it in an envelope and directed the nurse to send it to the friend whom he had entrusted with the other package. This was done.

Although every one was curious as to what the mysterious packets contained, not one of the children or friends dared to break the seals. No one desired to devote his life to something he could know nothing about until too late to recede. The envelopes were deposited in one of the banks of France. After I had studied for some years in Russia, Germany and the Orient, I decided to take up the work of my illustrious grandfather. I decided that what he had felt so important that he had so safeguarded it must be important enough to devote one's life to. In 1906 I took the vow and broke the seals. Within were a number of documents and photographs. The first paper said:

"Whoever opens this must solemnly swear to carry out the work which I have left unfinished. I have come to the conclusion that Atlantis was not only a great territory between America and the west coast of Africa and Europe, but the cradle of all our civilization as well. There has been much dispute between scientists on this matter. According to one group the tradition of Atlantis is purely fictional, founded upon fragmentary accounts of a Deluge some thousands of years before the Christian era. Others declare the tradition wholly historical, but incapable of absolute proof.

"In the included material records, notes and explanations are to be found, the proofs that exist in my mind of the matter. Whoever takes charge of this mission is solemnly obligated to continue my researches and to form a definite statement using as well the matter I leave with this and crediting me with my just dues in the discovery. A special fund is deposited in the Bank of France to be paid to the bearer of the enclosed receipt, and this should pay the expenses of the research. The Almighty be with this great effort.

"HEINRICH SCHLIEMANN."

I cannot in this limited space give all the papers--nor do I care to. But one of the most important from the narrative's standpoint read:

"When in 1873, I made the excavation of the ruins of Troy at Hissarlik and discovered in the Second City the famous 'Treasure of Priam,' I found among that treasure a peculiar bronze vase, of great size. Within it were several pieces of pottery, various small images of peculiar metal, coins of the same metal and objects made of fossilized bone. Some of these objects and the bronze vase were engraved with a sentence in Phoenician hieroglyphics. The sentence read 'From the King Chronos of Atlantis.'

You who read can imagine my excitement! Here was the first, the very first material evidence

(Column Two)

of that great continent whose legend has lived for ages throughout the world. This material I kept secret, eager to make it the basis of investigations which I felt would prove of infinitely more importance than the discovery of a hundred Troys. But first I had to finish the work in which I was engaged, and I was the more eager to do this because I felt that I was sure to find other objects which would bear directly upon the lost continent. I was rewarded for my faith as you will see in the document marked B.

"In 1883 I found the Louvre a collection of objects excavated from Tiahuanaca, in Central America. And among, these I discovered pieces of pottery of exactly the same shape and material and objects of fossilized bone which reproduced line for line those which I had found in the bronze vase of the 'Treasure of Priam'! The similarity could not be a coincidence.

The shapes and decorations were to complex for that. It is beyond the range of coincidence for two artists in such widely separated countries as Central America and Crete to make two vases--I mention only one of the objects--of exactly the same shape, the same size and with curious owls' heads arranged in just the same way on each.

"The Central American vases had no Phoenician characters upon them nor writing of any sort. I hurried away to examine again my own objects and by tests and exhaustive examinations became convinced that the inscriptions had been made by other hands after the objects themselves had been manufactured.

"I secured pieces of these simulacrums from Tiahaunaca and subjected them to chemical and microscopic analysis. These tests proved conclusively that both the Central American vases and those from Troy had been made from the same peculiar clay, and I learned later, further and definitively, that this clay does not exist, either in old Phoenicia nor in Central America!

"The metal objects I had analyzed, because I could not recognize what they were made of. The metal was unlike any I had ever seen. The chemical analysis showed the material to be platinum, aluminum and copper--a combination never before found in the remains of the ancients and unknown to-day!

"Objects then, perfectly similar and having unquestionably a common source were found in such widely separated countries as these. The objects themselves are not Phoenician, Mycenean nor Central American. What is the conclusion? That they came to both places from a common centre. The inscription on my objects gave that centre--It was Atlantis!

"That the objects were held in great veneration is shown from their presence among the 'Treasure of Priam' and the special receptacle that held them. Their character left no doubt that they were objects of sacred ceremonies and from the same temple. Were they the remains of a worship which had existed on

(Column Three)

Atlantis and which that great land had impressed upon colonies and countries as far apart as ancient Crete and Central America? Were these things sent out by the mother land just as Bibles are sent out to-day from Christendom--and as statutes of Isis and her altar paraphernalia were sent by Egypt to her colonies?

"This extraordinary discovery and my failing health induced me to push more rapidly my investigations. I found in the Museum at St. Petersburg one of the oldest papyrus rolls in existence. It was written in the reign of Pharaoh Sent, of the Second Dynasty, or 4,571 years B. C. It contains a description of how the Pharaoh sent out an expedition 'to the West' in search of traces of the 'Land of Atlantis,' whence '3,350 years ago the ancestors of the Egyptians arrived carrying with themselves all the wisdoms of their native lands.' The expedition returned after five years with the report that they had found neither people nor objects which could give them a clue as to the vanished land. Another papyrus, in the same museum, written by Manetho, the Egyptian historian, gives a reference of a period of '13,900 years as the reign of the sages of Atlantis.' The papyrus places this at the very beginning of Egyptian history; it approximates 16,000 years ago.

"An inscription which I excavated at the Lion Gate at Mycenae in Crete recites that Misor, from whom, according to the inscription, the Egyptians were descended, was the child of Taaut or Thoth, the God of History, and that Taaut was the emigrated son of a 'priest of Atlantis, who having fallen in love with a daughter of King Chronos, escaped and landed after many wanderings in Egypt.' He built the first temple at Sais and there taught the wisdom of his native land. This full inscription is most important, and I have kept it secret. You will find it among the papers marked D."

I cannot go further here into more than a small part of the enormous mass of evidence, and it is material evidence of this continent of Atlantis that my grandfather had collected. I must pass to the end of this remarkable document:

"One of the tables of my Trojan excavation gives also a medical treatise of the Egyptian priests--for there was communication between Crete and Egypt for many centuries--for the removal of cataract from the eye and ulcer from the intestines by means of surgery. I have read almost a similar formula in a Spanish manuscript in Berlin whose writer took it from an Aztec priest in Mexico. That priest had gotten it from an ancient Mayan manuscript.

"In coming to my conclusion I must say that neither the Egyptians nor the Mayan race that made the civilization of Central America before the Aztecs were great navigators. They had no ships to cross the Atlantic. Nor did they. We can dismiss the agency of the Phoenicians

(Column Four)

as a real link between the hemispheres. Yet the similarity of Egyptian and Mayan life and civilization is so perfect that it is impossible to think of it as an accident. We find no such accidents in nature or history. The only possibility is that there was, as the legend says, a great continent that connected what we now call the New World with what we call the old. Perhaps at this time what there was of Europe and America was populated with monsters. Africa possibly had a monkey-like negro race. Man in our sense had not overrun them. But there was a land where civilization as high as that we now know and perhaps higher was flourishing. Its outskirts were the edge of wilderness. It was Atlantis. From Atlantis came the colonies that settled Egypt and Central America.

I realized that I faced a serious problem indeed, despite all the astonishing evidence, greater far than any one dreams, left me by my grandfather. There were other notes and allusions to the material proofs which were in the secret safe in Paris, and besides these was the strict injunction that I should keep the matter secret until I had followed up his instructions and had finished my research.

For six years I have worked indefatigably in Egypt, in Central and South America and in all the archeological museums on the globe. I have discovered Atlantis, I have verified the existence of this great continent and the fact that from it sprang all the civilizations of historic times without a doubt.

In my research I have made a principle to retire to such a seclusion that no periodical could reach me, and no curiosity of the public could disturb me in this serious and important work. I shall pursue the same course until my book is finished. For these reasons I have avoided up to this time all notoriety, through the press and every association with any scientific expeditions. I am an individualist and will do the work in my individual way. However, I have been willing to follow the invitation of this newspaper and to reveal this secret of my illustrious grandfather and to give some of the facts which I have discovered and why I claim to be the discoverer of Atlantis. I proceed to what happened after I read Heinrich Schliemann's documents.

I at once proceeded to investigate the hidden collection in Paris. The owl headed vase was unique, of obviously extraordinarily ancient origin and on it I read the inscription in Phoenician characters: "From the King Chronos of Atlantis." I hesitated for days to break it for I still thought that the last letter of my grandfather might have been the result of a mind weakened by the approach of death. I could not see why it should be broken. It may be that he had found other vases of the kind of Hissarlik and had broken thme. He may have saved this last vase because he felt that

(Column Five)

an absolute proof of the evidence should be the possession of the one who should take up his work. I hesitate to write this because it seems to savor of pure romance. Yet it is absolute truth.

After all I broke it. I was not a little startled when out the bottom of the vase slipped a square of white, silver-like metal upon which were drawn strange figure and an inscription which were not like any hieroglyphs or writings I had ever seen. These were on the head side of the coin or medal. On the obverse side was engraved in ancient Phoenician, "Issued in the Temple of Transparent Walls." How did the metal get in the vase? I do not know. The neck was too small for its insertion, but there it was and it had been imbedded in the clay of the bottom and my grandfather had evidently known it was there.

If the vase was from Atlantis the piece must have come from it too. And yet my examination showed me that the Phoenician letters had been cut in after the object had been under the die that made the face figures. This is a mystery to me even now. But there is the evidence.

Besides this I found in the collection the other material objects which my grandfather had said came from Atlantis. One was a ring of the same peculiar metal as the coins or the medals. There was a strange looking elephant of fossilized bone, an extremely archaic vase and some other objects which I will not discuss now. The map by which the Egyptian captain had sought for Atlantis was there too. I prefer to save these other objects for my extended work--nor could I, under the instructions of my grandfather, tell of them. It is sufficient to say that no scientist can controvert them. The owl vase, the archaic vase, the bronze vase and the ring have the Phoenician inscription. The elephant and coins did not.

My grandfather had written that I should first pay attention to the ruins of the Temple of Sais and the Chucuna Valley in America. I arrived first in Egypt and started to excavate around the ruins of Sais. I worked a long time in vain. I found interesting pieces of antique ceremonial and astronomical uses, but no traces of what I wanted.

But one day, I made the acquaintance of an Egyptian hunter, who showed me a collection of old medals he had found in a sarcophagus in one of the tombs near by. Who can describe my surprise in finding among his collection two of the same design and size of the white medal I had found in the vase of Troy? The figures were not so lain of detail and the inscription was lacking, but they were undoubtedly of the same original as of mine. I procured them from the hunter and I investigated the sarcophagus. It proved to be that of a priest of the First Dynasty! One of the most ancient. But there was nothing else there of interest--to me.

Yet was I not progressing? Here was the coin in the vase of Troy, which, if my grandfather was right, came from Atlantis. And here were two of the same kind in a sarcophagus of a priest of the First Dynasty of the Temple of Sais, the temple which held the records of Atlantis and whose priest had recited them to Solon--their temple which had been founded by a son of Atlantis who had run away with a "daughter of Chronos," the name of which was on the vase of Hissarlik that held the coin! How explain?

I called to my aid two great French geological experts, and we examined the west coast of Africa at the points where my grandfather had indicated where he had believed the ancient Atlantis had touched that land. We

(Column Six)

found the whole shore here covered with volcanic action. Some distance in from the shore those evidences stopped. For many miles it was as though the volcanic action had chopped away land from the coast. Here I found an object of inestimable value to my research. It was a head of a child done in the same metal as that which formed the ring and the medals. It was imbedded in an encrustation of volcanic rock of great age. The chemical analysis showed it to be of exactly the same strange alloy I have described.

The full results of this survey I cannot go into here. They were immensely important, and they are supported by other testimony than my own.

(Column Seven)

I went to Paris and sought the owner of the Central American collection which my grandfather had alluded to. He consented that I break his owl headed vase for the purpose of investigation. I broke the vase.

And out of it slipped a medal exactly the same size and material as the three I had! The only difference was in the arrangement of the hieroglyphs!

Here there were three links: The coins in my grandfather's secret collection. The coin in the Atlantis vase. The coins in the Egyptian sarcophagus. The coin in the vase from Central America. The head from the Moroccan Coast!

I at once went to Central America, to Mexico and to Peru. I have dug up graveyards and excavated in the cities. The cemetery of the Chucuna Valley, where the ancient Chimus are buried, gave me immense material for other clues. I will say that although I found fragments of the owl-headed vases, I found no more medals there. But what I did find was just as important. These are inscriptions which will startle the world. And I found other medals at the Pyramid of Teohuatican in Mexico of the same alloy, but with different script!

I have reasons for saying that the strange medals were used as money in Atlantis forty thousand years ago. These reasons are based not only on my own researches, but upon those of my grandfather which I have not mentioned.

(Column Eight)

The "Temple of Transparent Walls" was one of the National Treasuries of the Lost Continent. As the Atlanteans and after them the Egyptians, the Mayans and the Chimus were hieratic nations, it is natural that a temple was considered as the centre and foundation of social, political life as well as the cradle of art, science, education and religion. Among the facts that I have to reveal in my book there are clear indications that of the City of the Golden Gates, as it was called, and two clear references to the Temple of Transparent Walls.

The Atlantean Temple of Transparent Walls was usually a high public place. Its operations were open for the masses. Did the words "transparent" have a symbolic meaning or did there really exist a temple with transparent walls? I do not know. However, I can prove that the Phoenicians got there knowledge of glass making from the "people who lived beyond the pillars of Hercules." It is necessary to say that the country which used the ancient medals as an equivalent of labor had a more advanced currency system than we have at present.

I pass, for lack of space, over the hieroglyphics and other evidences which I have

(Column Nine)

discovered that show that the civilizations of Egypt, of Mycenae, of Central America, South America and the Mediterranean had a common origin. They will be incontrovertible". I pass on to the translation of a Maya manuscript which is part of the famous collection of Le Plongeon, the Troano manuscript. It can be seen in the British Museum. It reads:

"In the year of 6 Kan, on the 11 Muluc, in the Month Zac, there occured terrific earthquakes which continued without interruption until the 13 Chuen. The country of the hills of mud, the Land of Mu, was sacrificed. Being twice upheaved it disappeared during the night, being continually shaken by the fires of the under earth. Being confined these caused the land to sink and rise several times and in various places. At last the surface gave way, and then ten countries were torn asunder and scattered. They sank with their 64,000,000 of inhabitants 8,000 years before the writing of this book."

In the records of the old Buddhistic Temple at Lhasa there is to be seen an ancient Chaldean inscription written about 2,000 years B.C. It reads:

"When the star Bal fell on the place where is now only sea and sky the Seven Cities with their Golden Gates and Transparent Temples quivered and shook like the leaves of a tree in storm. And behold a flood of fire and smoke arose from the palaces. Agony and cries of the multitude filled the air. They sought refuge in their temples and citadels. And the wise Mu, the hieratic of Ra-Mu, arose and said to them: 'Did not I predict all this?' And the women and the men in their precious stones and shining garments lamented: 'Mu, save us.' And Mu replied: 'You shall die together with your slaves and your riches and from your ashes will arise new nations. If they forget they are superior, not because of what they put on, but of what they put out, the same lot will befall them!' Flame and smoke choked the words of Mu. The land and its inhabitants were torn to pieces and swallowed by the depths in a few months."

How account for these two stories--one from Thibet, the other from Central America, each mentioning the same cataclysm and each referring to the land of Mu?

When I throw open all the facts that I have, there will be no mystery about it.

Let me now go back for a moment to that document of my grandfather which I have quoted and which was the basis of my research. After telling of the inscription which

(Column Ten)

he had found in the Dome Tombs of Mycenae, he continued:

"The religion of Egypt was pre-eminently sun worship. Ra was the sun god of the Egyptians. The religion of the Mayas in Central America was the same. Ra-Na was the sun god of the ancient Peruvians.

"My long archeological studies of various nations have proven that all of them show their earliest childhood and maturity. But I have failed to find any traces of a rude and savage Egypt or a rude, barbarous Maya race. I have found both these nations mature in their very earliest period, skilful, strong and learned. I have never found a time when they lacked in ability to organize their labor nor lacking in ability to dig canals, build highways, pyramids and temples, to irrigate fields nor a time when they did not know medicine, astronomy and the principles of highly organized government. Like the Mayas the Egyptians practised monogamy, and they built their cities and temples in the same style, exhibiting a technical knowledge and skill that remains a puzzle to the engineers of this age. Neither Egyptians nor Mayans were a black race, but yellow. Both nations had slaves and an intellectual caste, but the relations between the classes were cordial and humane. Their basic principles of government were the same.

"Lepsius found the same sacred symbols in the ceremonials of the Egyptians as in the Peruvians. Le Plongeon, the great French archeologist, recovered at Chichen-Itza in Yucatan the figure of a god who was club-footed and bore in every way the attributes of the great god Thoth, of the Egyptians!

"In the Egyptian and the American pyramids the outside was covered with a thick coating of smooth and shining cement of such strength as our builders are unable to get. Humboldt considered the Pyramid of Cholula of the same type as the Temple of Jupiter at Belus.

"In both America and Egypt, the pyramids were built in the same style. I have found the pyramids on both sides of the Atlantic with their four sides pointing astronomically like the arms of the cross, in the same directions. In both the line through their centres is on the astronomical meridian. The construction in grades and steps is the same and in both cases the larger pyramids are dedicated to the sun."

WHAT THE LOST ATLANTIS IS SUPPOSED TO HAVE BEEN

A GREAT island in the Atlantic opposite the Mediterranean; the remnant of a mighty continent which once reached from the west coast of Africa and Europe to the shores of Central America. The ancient world had a clear tradition of it.

It was utterly destroyed in a day and a nigh by cataclysmic volcanic outbursts and sank beneath the sea with all except a few of its millions of inhabitants.

It was the region where mankind first rose from barbarism to a civilization more advanced than that of ours today.

It became in the course of hundreds of thousands of years a world-conquering nation. It colonized Egypt, the west coast of Africa and Europe, Central America, the shores of the Gulf of Mexico, the Mississippi Valley, the Pacific Coast of South America, the Mediterranean, the Baltic, the Black Sea and the Caspian. It was the cradle of civilization, and the civilization of the ancient world and our civilization today are direct shoots of the Atlantic culture.

The racial memory of Atlantis is found in the legends of the Garden of Eden of the Bible, the Garden of the Hesperides of the Greeks, the Asgard of the Scandinavians, the Tir n'Og of the Celts and in all the legends of a wonderful, mysterious land in which dwelt gods or godlike mortals.

The stories of the Deluge, versions of which are found in the traditions of almost every ancient and modern race, are simply the memory of the stupendous catastrophe which wiped out Atlantis, the tale of which was carried by those who escaped to all the lost land's colonies--and these represented all the civilization of the world at that time.

In the same way the escape of some of the Atlanteans over a narrow land bridge, which connected Atlantis with what is now Brittany, survives in the legends of the Rainbow Bridge Perilous with the razor edge which the Scandinavians believed was the only road to Asgard, the dwelling place of the gods, in the famous Hell's Causway of the religious books of the Middle Ages and in similar legends of the Hindoos, the Mayans and the Turanians.

The gods and goddesses of the ancient Greeks, the Phoenicians, Hindoos and Scandinavians were simply the Kings, Queens and heroes of Atlantis, and the acts attributed to them in mythology are a confused recollection of real historical events.

The religions of Egypt, Peru and that of the Mayans, the vanished race that built the buried cities of Central America, and upon the wrecks of whose civilization the Aztecs built their empire, were the original religion of Atlantis.

The oldest colony formed by Atlantis was Egypt, whose civilization was a provincial reproduction of that of the mother country. The next oldest were those of Peru and Central America.

The Phoenician alphabet, parent of all the European alphabets, was derived from and Atlantis alphabet, which was also conveyed from Atlantis to the Mayans. The symbols and hieroglyphics of both Egypt and the Mayans came from the same source, and so is explained their similarity, to great to be accidental.

Atlantis was the original site of the Indo-European family of nations, as well as the Semitic and possibly the Turanian.

The Atlanteans had full knowledge of electricity, steam and other natural forces. They had also aeroplanes, power ships and explosives. They were prodigious engineers and the first workers of iron. They used gold and silver and a vanished precious metal known as orichalcum in enormous quantities for ornamentation.

WHO DR. HEINRICH SCHLIEMANN WAS AND THE TREASURES HE FOUND

HEINRICH Schliemann whose work was to give a new impetus to the study of Greek origins and to be the beginning of the revelation of an unknown world of ancient days, was born at Neu-Bucknow, Mecklenburg-Schwerin, Germany, on January 6, 1822. He was the son of a country minister. When he was barely seven years old, he received a child's history of the world in which the picture of the destruction of Troy made a profound impression on him. At that age he vowed to search those sites when "he was rich." By the time he was ten he had produced a prize-winning essay on the Trojan War.

But his father was poor, and Schliemann, for all his dreams, had to work prosaically. In St. Petersburg, during the Crimean War, he married secretly a Russian noblewoman. Through her he became a buying agent of the Russian army and made a fortune. In 1850 he was forced to leave Russia, came to America, went to California and became an American citizen. He made a second fortune in America, and in 1868 started to Greece to fulfil his ambitions.

Brilliant beyond any other archaeologist of his time, and filled with curious intuitions that ran counter to current beliefs and which were uncanny in their accuracy, he met with instant success. One of his learned compeers has said of him that "If it did not seem so absurd, one might say that Schliemann is an incarnation of some ancient Mycenean, and remembers just where to look." At any rate he began to cut the soil from Hissarilk in 1870, and in 1873 he discovered the "Great Treasure of Priam." It has always been said that Schliemann did not reveal all of this treasure, and this wonderful story of his grandson confirms this.

Schliemann started at the virgin soil, and of course, the first city he found was the oldest. It was in the second city that he fond the treasure. This city he though was ancient Troy. But above this were the remains of seven other cities.

It was afterward proven that the sixth, city above the second was really ancient Troy! The second city was immensely more ancient, and very conservatively, its destruction may be placed at 20,000 B. C.! It had been a very great city, with Cyclopean architecture and a high grade of civilization. All this is immensely important in view of the announcement of the "Chronos of Atlantis" vase found there. The priests of Sais told Solon that Atlantis had been destroyed 9,000 years before their conversation. This would seem to prove that the second city of Schilemann was actually the metropolis of an Atlantean colony, and that the mother country was still existing at the time the Treasure was placed in the second city!

A dispute with the Turkish Government over the Treasure stopped his Hissarlik work, and he turned his attention to Mycenae, on the Island of Crete, the historic capital of Agamemnon of the Iliad. He excavated the wonderful Lion Gate, the famous Shaft Tombs and Dome Tombs, but not till now has the news of the Atlantean inscription he found in the Dome Tombs been made public. He found, too, in the Shaft Tombs the most remarkable hoard of treasure that ever greeted the eye of a discoverer.

In them was gold in profusion. It was beaten into face masks and wrought into hundreds of articles.

It can be said that in this treasure were other vastly more precious objects having a direct bearing upon Atlantis, which Dr. Schliemann kept secret, as he had his discoveries in the second city. What these were will be told in due time by his grandson.

The other extraordinary discoveries of Dr. Schliemann in Crete can be found in the records. In 1890 he died.

This brief sketch is necessary to explain how great and authority and discoverer was the man whose grandson speaks in these pages, and to show upon what real foundations this article, whose astonishing claims are bound to raise some incredulity, is based.

www.ingramcontent.com/pod-product-compliance
Lightning Source LLC
Chambersburg PA
CBHW051554010526
44118CB00022B/2710